Robert E. Lee

Robert E. Lee

A Play by John Drinkwater

London: Sidgwick & Jackson, Ltd.
3 Adam Street, Adelphi.   1923

First published in 1923.

All Dramatic Rights reserved by the Author.

To

DAVID

ROBERT E. LEE

SCENE I.

The morning of April 18th, 1861.

The room of GENERAL SCOTT, *Commander-in-Chief of the United States Army, at the War Office, Washington.*

At a side-table an OFFICER *is writing. After a few moments he rings a bell, and an* ORDERLY *comes in.*

The Officer: This clock has stopped. That's twice in a week. Why don't you keep it wound up?

The Orderly (winding it): I'm sorry, sir.

The Officer: Yes. It's no use if it doesn't go, is it?

The Orderly: No, sir.

The Officer: No. Take that to the people in Room 26 (*giving a paper*). What time is Colonel Lee's appointment?

The Orderly (consulting a pad): Twelve o'clock, sir.

The Officer: What's the time now?

The Orderly (looking at the clock in his hand): About —I don't exactly know, sir.

The Officer: That's just it. You should keep it wound up. Let me know. Where's the General?

The Orderly : I believe he's washing his face, sir.

The Officer (*in parenthesis*) : He's always washing his face.

The Orderly : Yes, sir.

The Officer : Don't be insubordinate.   Let me know the time.   (*As the* ORDERLY *is going*) By the way, you come from Alabama, don't you ?

The Orderly : Yes, sir.

The Officer : Then you ought to know better.

The Orderly : I beg your pardon, sir ?

The Officer : You've seceded.

The Orderly : I have, sir ?

The Officer : Your state has, sir.   That's the sixth. Word has come this morning.   What do you mean by it ?

The Orderly : That's very awkward.

The Officer : What shall you do ?

The Orderly : I don't know, sir.   I mean—I don't want to go away—but, you see, I come from Alabama, sir.   It's going to be very difficult.

The Officer : Rebellion, that's what it is.

The Orderly : I don't want to rebel, sir.

The Officer : Alabama does.

The Orderly : Of course, if you put it like that, sir, I'm sure I don't know.   I've a kind of a faith in Alabama.

The Officer : You're a soldier of the United States.

The Orderly : I know, sir.   But Alabama.   Do you think I ought to fight against Alabama, sir ? You see, I come from there.

The Officer : It is not for me to decide.

The Orderly: No, sir. I shall have to decide for myself. I see that.

The Officer: Put the clock right.

The Orderly: Yes, sir. (*He goes, taking the clock.*)

> The OFFICER *takes some papers from his table to the* GENERAL'S. *As he is arranging them,* GENERAL SCOTT *appears at the door, where he turns and speaks into the room beyond.*

Scott: Empson, send that blackboard in.

> *The answer comes, 'Yes, sir.'*

Scott: Dirty place this office, Perrin.

The Officer (*referring to his hands*): I can't say I've noticed it, sir.

Scott: Very dirty. Have to keep on washing.

> *The* ORDERLY *comes in, with a blackboard and easel, and the clock.*

Scott: There.

> *The* ORDERLY *places the blackboard above* SCOTT'S *table, and the clock on the* OFFICER'S, *and goes.*
>
> *On the blackboard is a rough outline map of the twenty-nine states of the Union, with five of them, South Carolina, Mississippi, Florida, Georgia, and Louisiana, marked off with a chalk cross. To these* SCOTT *now adds another, marking off Alabama.*

Scott: Alabama. That's bad.

The Officer: There's no word from Virginia yet, sir.

Scott: They were still in session last night. We may hear at any moment.

The Officer: If they go, it will be a long business.

Scott : Two years wouldn't settle it, Perrin.

The Officer (*indicating paper*) : The recruiting reports are good this morning, sir.   Over half the President's seventy-five thousand in three days.

Scott (*consulting the papers on his table*) : Yes—yes. What's the time ?

The Officer : Just on twelve o'clock, sir.

Scott : If Virginia goes, we shall lose Lee.

The Officer : Surely not, sir.   A soldier all his life.

Scott : I hope not, but I think so.

The ORDERLY *comes in.*

The Orderly : Colonel Lee is here, sir.

Scott : Ask him to come in.

The ORDERLY *goes.*

Scott : You needn't go, Perrin.   Take notes.

Perrin : Yes, sir.

The ORDERLY *shows in* ROBERT E. LEE, *at this time a Lieutenant-Colonel in the United States Army.   The* ORDERLY *goes.*

Scott : Good-morning, Colonel.

Lee : Good-morning, sir.

Scott : This is Major Perrin.   You've no objection to his hearing what we have to say ?

Lee : No, certainly.

Scott : Sit down, please.

They sit.

Scott : It is at the President's suggestion that I asked you to come.

Lee : I am honoured, sir.

Scott : The problem is at the moment common— lamentably common.   But we felt that your case was

a special one, or, rather, in a special sense a representative one. The esteem in which you stand in
Virginia, and your personal record in the army, make
your views of particular—as I say of representative
—importance. We considered that a personal inter-
view was the proper way of learning them.

Lee: I welcome your confidence.

Scott: You are aware that six states have already
declared for secession from the Union?

Lee: I understood five.

Scott: Alabama's decision comes this morning.

Lee: I had not heard.

Scott: Do you approve?

Lee: If I were a mere spectator of events, I should
say no.

Scott: A spectator?

Lee: It can hardly be an abstract question with
me, you see, sir.

Scott: You mean Virginia?

Lee: Being a Virginian, yes, sir.

Scott: Your state, you mean, right or wrong?

Lee: Right and wrong are such dangerous words
for men to use, ever.

Scott: Duty is a plain thing, Colonel Lee.

Lee: It should be, sir. But for it we may have to
forfeit the good opinion of men that we cherish. My
duty may not seem to me, for example, what you
consider it should mean.

Scott: Your mind is fixed?

Lee: No—it is very gravely troubled.

Scott: Virginia's decision is not yet announced.

Lee: The Convention was sitting late into the night, I hear.

Scott: I gather that the indications are that she will follow the others.

Lee: In view of what has happened, I fear so.

Scott: You fear so?

Lee: Yes. I am opposed to secession on principle. More, I do not think the issue upon which it is proposed a sufficient one. I would gladly see every slave freed rather than that the Union should be broken.

Scott: You hold your commission under that Union.

Lee: I know, sir. It has made my life a fortunate one.

Scott: Then where can be the difference in opinion of which you speak?

Lee: I am two things, sir. I am not a statesman, nor do I in any other way control public policy. I am a soldier. But before that I am a citizen of Virginia. If my state decides to dispute the authority of the service in which I have for so long had the honour to be, I may regret the decision, but I may feel it my duty to respect it in my action.

Scott: Then let me put it more explicitly. The Government, as you know, has declared war on the rebel states.

Lee: The seceding states.

Scott: The rebel states, Colonel Lee. Be plain about that. Major Anderson has been forced to surrender at Fort Sumter. The President's appeal for seventy-five thousand men is being answered eagerly. We are facing no holiday campaign. Other states will doubtless join the rebels. Two years will hardly see it through.

Lee: I should have said four, sir.

Scott: I was discussing the situation as a whole with President Lincoln yesterday evening. You were much spoken of. There is no officer in the army of whom he has a higher opinion, and I was privileged to say how just I considered that opinion to be. He instructed me to offer you the command of all Union forces in the field. I may say for myself that I think that even so great a distinction has been fully earned, Colonel Lee, and I could make the offer to no one with so much satisfaction.

Lee: The President's confidence, and yours, sir, are very much above my merit. I cannot express my sense of this. But what am I to say?

Scott: To say? How do you mean, to say?

Lee: Virginia has not spoken.

Scott: The army that you serve calls you to lead it. And you ask what you shall say.

Lee: To lead it against whom?

Scott: Against rebels to their country.

Lee: It may be against Virginia.

Scott: Then still against rebels.

Lee: Against my own people.

Scott: You are a soldier, you say. You are under orders.

Lee: I have been allowed to serve under you, sir. I know what discipline is—I do not need to be reminded. There have been times when I have obeyed orders with no very light heart. When I arrested John Brown at Harper's Ferry, I could have wished that the duty had fallen to another. For I believed the old man had conscience in him. But then obedience was against my private feelings only. Now it may be against my public loyalty to the soil that made me. My Virginia. You may be asking me to invade, perhaps to destroy my own homeland. Do you wonder that I answer 'What am I to say'?

Scott: Suppose Virginia to stand with the Union?

Lee: It is unlikely. But then I am merely a Lieutenant-Colonel.

Scott: And otherwise?

Lee: I think I should have to offer my resignation. I should ask for twenty-four hours in which to decide. But I can see but one conclusion open to me.

There is a knock at the door.

Scott: What's that? See what it is, Perrin.

PERRIN, *who has been making his notes, goes to the door. The* ORDERLY *is there.*

The Orderly: This has just been brought from the White House, sir. It was to be given to the General at once.

Perrin: All right.

The ORDERLY *goes;* PERRIN *gives a letter to* SCOTT, *and returns to his table.*

Scott (after reading): It is from the President. Virginia has declared for secession.

Lee (after a pause, rising): Virginia. Fifty-three

years of age. I beg your pardon, sir. Is there anything else to say?

Scott: Thirty of those years you have been a
gallant soldier, Colonel Lee. I do not forget our
days in Mexico together. Think of them, too. It
would be a hard day should you turn rebel—no, it's
the only word. (*Rising*) You have your twenty-four
hours.

Lee: Thank you, sir. I do not accept the word,
and I can foresee but one answer. But I thank you,
and I shall care deeply for your respect if I can
keep it.

Scott (*shaking hands*) : Good-bye.

Lee: Good-bye, sir.

      PERRIN *opens the door, and* LEE *goes.*

Scott: That's the best soldier in America to-day.

Perrin: Why don't you arrest him, sir?

Scott: Don't be a damned fool, Perrin.

Perrin: Certainly, sir.

Scott (*marking Virginia with a cross on the blackboard*): That's worst of all. Ask McClellan, Bryce,
and Simpson to meet me here at three o'clock this
afternoon. I've got chalk all over myself. I must
go and wash. (*He goes.*)

      PERRIN *takes some papers from* SCOTT'S *table
      to his own and rings the bell.* The ORDERLY
      comes in.*

The Orderly: Yes, sir?

Perrin: Find out at once where Generals McClellan and Bryce and Colonel Simpson are, and let me
know. And take that blackboard back.

2

The Orderly : Yes, sir.   (*He goes to the blackboard. As he is about to lift it*—) Virginia, sir ?   Has Virginia gone too, sir ?

Perrin : It looks as though it might be so.

The Orderly : But Colonel Lee is a Virginian.

Perrin : Well, what of that ?

The Orderly : Is he going to be a rebel too, sir ?

Perrin : Take the blackboard away, and do as I told you.

The Orderly : I wish I could speak to Colonel Lee. It's going to be a very difficult matter.   I beg your pardon, sir.   (*He goes, taking the blackboard.*)

Perrin (*back at his papers, after a moment, in interrogation*) : Don't be a damned fool, Perrin ?

THE SCENE CLOSES.

Scene II.

In the woods near Arlington, Virginia. Early after-noon of the same day.

Warmly dressed, and seated around a wood fire, three young hunters are finishing their mid-day meal. They are Tom Buchanan, *six foot two, a white hope of the sixties, if such things were wanted then, and his inclinations had turned to the Fancy, twenty-two years or so of age, side-whiskers, and all genial-ity ;* Ray Warrenton, *of the same age, the heir of one of the First Families of Virginia, and not unpleasantly aware of it, very elegant, his good form a touch self-conscious but still good; and* David Peel, *rather older, a dreamer who no more con-fuses dreaming with stupor than he does over-emphasis with passion.*

Buchanan : It's been a good trip.   You never shot better, David.

Peel : I don't know that I wouldn't just as soon miss.

Warrenton : I thought we all shot rather well.

Buchanan : Well, we may all need to before long.

Warrenton : I suppose it's all known by now.

Buchanan : I expect your father was right.

Warrenton : Yes, we shall be in it sure enough.   He said he should certainly vote for seceding at the convention.   In fact, all the Warrentons feel that about it.

Peel : Of course, if the Warrentons say so.

Warrenton: They've had a good deal to do with making Virginia, you can't get over that.

Peel: Ego et rex meus, eh?

Warrenton: What's he talking about?

Buchanan: Never mind, Ray. Warrentons for ever.

Warrenton: That's just what they will be. As it was in the beginning—but what does he mean about rex meus?

Peel: Golden lads and girls all must—perhaps not the Warrentons, though.

Warrenton: You know, David, you're the sort of fellow who ought to have discouraged Christopher Columbus.

Buchanan: I wonder whether they've sent for Colonel Lee at Washington yet.

Warrenton: My father said they were sure to at once.

Buchanan: Perhaps we shall hear about it to-night.

Peel: I shouldn't be surprised if the party is off.

Buchanan: What do you suppose he will do?

Warrenton: Lee of Virginia? What Virginia does, of course.

Buchanan: I saw him at Arlington a month ago. He didn't think there was any chance of trouble then.

Peel: There oughtn't to have been any chance. We ought to have got together over it somehow. These political fellows will do anything with you.

Warrenton: But you can't have Washington interfering like that. Slavery is part of the Constitution, anyway.

Peel: Well, it's no good arguing about it.

Buchanan: I see what Ray means, though.

Peel: I see what he means, but where's the sense in killing each other about it ? The question will still be there when half of us are shot to pieces.

Buchanan: Well, we don't want to fight.

Warrenton : We only ask to be let alone.

Peel : Mr. Lincoln doesn't see it like that.

Warrenton : But what does Mr. Lincoln know about Virginia ?

Peel : He happens to be President.

Buchanan: You don't know that. We may be out of it by now.

Warrenton : Quite right, too, if we are. The Warrentons have been at Mount Weston a hundred and seventy years. What can the backwoods of Illinois know about people like that ?

Peel: A hundred and seventy years. There was a battle at Marathon once. I believe that was even longer ago.

Warrenton : Yes, but Mr. Lincoln didn't interfere with that, and we aren't at Marathon, anyway.

Buchanan: David doesn't mean anything.

Warrenton : I don't suppose he does. It doesn't sound like it.

Peel : But we can't get over the opinion of a man like Mr. Lincoln so easily.

Warrenton: If his opinion is that he can treat Virginians like schoolboys, he ought to keep it to himself.

Peel : Have you seen him ?

Warrenton: No, and I don't want to.

Peel: I heard his Inaugural. There's something great about him.

Buchanan: You talk as though you thought we ought to give in.

Peel: No. I don't really know enough about it. I only feel that the people who do know ought somehow to understand each other, and keep things straight.

Buchanan: But if Virginia went out, you wouldn't hesitate?

Peel: Of course I shouldn't. As far as that goes, we're in for a war on one side or the other whatever Virginia does. Some of them are certain to go. Virginia in particular doesn't seem to me to matter so much.

Warrenton: What are you talking about—of course Virginia matters.

Peel: You're not very quick sometimes, Ray.

Warrenton: Well, I'm going to be quick about this. If Virginia is out, I'm in the army to-morrow.

Buchanan: Naturally, we shall all be that.

Peel: Yes, we shall all be that.

Buchanan: It will be a great thing.

Peel: Like shooting straight—and yet——

Warrenton: Two Warrentons were with George Washington at Yorktown.

Buchanan: I've heard them say that Colonel Lee is the best brain in the Army. Mr. Lincoln won't want to lose him.

Warrenton: But he will. Lee for Virginia—don't

you make any mistake about that.   He'll be a man to follow.

Peel: It will be bare feet before we finish—if we live to the finish.

Warrenton: Nonsense.   They'll just beat against us till they are tired out.   And who knows, we may smash Washington itself.

Peel: Oh, we shall fight well enough, as well as they, better if you like.   But I see it all ahead—one year, two, three, perhaps four.   And we shall win to-day, and to-day.   There's good blood in us, we shall become another wonder of the world, Warrentons and the rest of us.   And then always to-morrow we shall wake up, and see them, the beaten ones, before us, stronger and bigger than ever.   And so it will go on.   And our clothes will wear out, and we shall be hungry, and we shall have nothing to shoot straight with any more.   And there will be just graves, and a story, and America.

Warrenton: Here, I say—you're pretty dismal, David.

Buchanan: Well, it's worth coming to bare feet for, anyway.

Peel: Yes, it's worth it.   Once thinking is over, it's worth it—that's the mystery.

Warrenton: I don't see any mystery.   It's just a plain quarrel, and it's an old way of settling it.

Peel: Old—and strange.

Warrenton: Well, I don't see it.

Buchanan: We ought to be going.   It will take us two hours yet, and they want us to be at Arlington

Heights by seven.   Where's Duff?   (*He calls into the woods*) Duff—Duff!   (*He calls in the other direction*) Duff—Du—u—u—f!

> *The others are preparing to start. For a few moments there is no answer to* BUCHANAN'S *call. Then in the distance is heard a banjo, and the tune of 'Dixie's Land.'*

Buchanan (*calling again*): Duff.

A voice (*in the distance, the banjo still playing*): Coming.

> *The banjo comes rapidly nearer, while knapsacks and rifles are gathered up.*

Buchanan: Duff will take his banjo to the war with him.

Warrenton: Yes—what's that about music? Some poet said it, didn't he? Something about savages.

Peel: Don't you have anything to do with them, Ray.   They'll upset you.

Warrenton: What, savages?

Peel: No, poets.

Warrenton: Honestly, though, what's the use of them?

Peel: I couldn't tell you.

Warrenton: I'm not clever enough, you mean,   I had an aunt, though, who used to read one of them. Hemans, I think his name was.

Peel: Mrs. Hemans.

Warrenton: Good Lord, do women do it too?

Peel: Your type's a very persistent one, Ray.

Warrenton: I suppose that's meant to be no compliment either.

The banjo arrives. Its player is DUFF PEN-
NER, *a black-haired, stockish young man, whose
chief concern in life is to use up an inexhaustible
supply of energy and good spirits. He has been
sent into the woods to play his banjo by himself.*

Penner : Time to go, time to go, and here's the
fellow on the old banjo.

Buchanan : I've told you before about that.

Penner : Go on telling, Tom my boy. I've thought
it all out—played it out, you might say, played it
out as clear as moonshine or a split apple. Virginia, I said, are you going to give way ? And No,
said Virginia, no, Duff, no, not on your life and
your old banjo. So I'm for a soldier. I shall say
to Colonel Lee to-night, ' Colonel, I'm for a soldier.'
Now, boys, we're all for soldiers, aren't we ?

Peel : We're all for soldiers, Duff.

Penner : Then let us all say to Colonel Lee,
' Colonel, we're all for soldiers, and we want to be
with you, and we want to be together.'

Buchanan : That's good, Duff. Together is good.
Shall we ?

Peel : Must the banjo go too ?

Penner : David Peel, your name may be David,
but you're a Philistine.

Warrenton : That's it, that's just what he is. Put
that with your ' rex meus.'

Peel : Admirable banjo. I dare say we shall need
it. Banjos won't be common.

Warrenton : You know, that sounds simple enough,
but I can't understand even that.

Peel: I'm sorry. I mean to be plain.

Warrenton : It seems to me you're always flitting round the corner.

Peel : There aren't many straight roads for us.

Warrenton : There you are again. I find plenty.

Buchanan : Straight or twisting, we shall be together, though.

Penner (*strumming*) :

      We're going for soldiers,
        For soldiers we will go—
      Duff and David, Thomas and Ray,
        Playing on the old banjo.

Peel : No more hunting—for which of us, I wonder.

Buchanan : Don't think things like that, David.

Peel : They think themselves, don't they ?

Warrenton : We've just got to think one thing— hit and hit hard.

Peel : Don't worry about me, Ray.

Buchanan : Come along. All ready ?

Penner : To the tune of Dixie. By orders of the day.

    He plays 'Dixie's Land', and he, BUCHANAN, *and* WARRENTON *sing the words* :

'To the land, to the land, to the land, to the land, I wish I was in Dixie.'

    While they are doing so, PEEL *is gazing into the valley, in the direction they are going.*

Peel : Ssh !

Buchanan : What is it, David ?

    They stop singing.

Peel : There. Do you see him ?

He slowly raises his rifle, aims, and fires.

Buchanan : By thunder ! That's deadly. Four hundred yards if it's a foot.

Penner : I'm on your side, David, not a doubt of it.

Peel : We can pick him up. Where did you tell them to wait, Tom ?

Buchanan : Just down the road.

Peel : Good.

Penner : By order, as I said.

He plays again, and they all go, singing ' Dixie.'

THE SCENE CLOSES.

Scene III.

The evening of the same day.

A room at the Lee House, Arlington Heights, brightly lit and cordial. It looks out on to a verandah, supported on the far side by the large columns of early colonial architecture. From these we should look across falling ground, down to the Potomac River. The windows are closed, but the clear spring night can be seen through them, the curtains being drawn to show the coloured lanterns that are hung on the verandah.

A door of the room is open, to a room beyond, from which comes the sound of dance music. Mr. Stean, *a man of forty-five, dances into the room with his partner, followed by* Ray Warrenton *and his. They go round the room and out of it, and two other couples, the men being* Duff Penner *and* Tom Buchanan, *follow them, dancing.* Buchanan *and his partner stop.*

The Girl: Shall we sit down?

Buchanan: Yes, let us.

> *They do so.* Penner *and his partner complete the round and go out.*

Girl: I think it's wonderful of Colonel Lee, don't you?

Buchanan: You mean dancing to-night?

Girl: Yes.

Buchanan: I wonder what he will say.

Girl: Mrs. Lee tells me his answer has to be given by twelve o'clock to-morrow.

They go on talking as PENNER *and his partner dance in again, laughing.*

Penner (*stopping in front of* BUCHANAN) : I say, Tom, Elizabeth says that if you go soldiering I've got to take care of you.

Buchanan (*rising*) : That's very comforting. He's going to take his banjo, Betty.

Elizabeth (*sitting*) : You speak as though it were all settled.

Girl : I don't see what can stop it now, after this morning's declaration. We're really at war now, aren't we, Mr. Buchanan ?

Buchanan : There's no official answer from Washington to our note yet. But it comes to that. We shall hear by the morning.

DAVID PEEL *comes in with his partner, and is followed a moment later by* COLONEL LEE *and his,* MRS. STEAN. *When they are halfway round the room the dance finishes.* PEEL *and his partner join* BUCHANAN *and the others.* LEE *takes his partner to a seat by the window, and stands looking out. The other group talks.*

Lee : Thank you. I must say a waltz is best of all.

His Partner : And that's a beautiful tune. It's very good of you to dance at all to-night, Colonel. John and I quite expected to be put off.

Lee : There will be so much to put off, you see. It seemed a pity to spoil what may be the last chance —or, the last for a long time. Besides, I was thinking of myself. I like dancing. It composes me.

His Partner : I suppose one mustn't be inquisitive ?

Lee: As to—— ?

His Partner: What is happening.

Lee: I think you know as much as I do. We have seceded, that's all.

His Partner: But you yourself?

Lee: That can't be very important.

His Partner: Come now, Colonel, you know it is very important, or if you don't, everybody else does.

Lee: No, no. If I resign, I'm merely a citizen of Virginia.

His Partner: Everybody knows that the South is sure to offer you something high up.

Lee: I don't seek it.

His Partner: It's desperately troubling. What do you think John ought to do? Of course, he has lived in Virginia for fifteen years, but he belongs to Massachusetts at heart.

Lee: Yes, that's bad. How can I advise, or anybody? Each man will have to decide for himself.

His Partner: Somebody told him this afternoon that General Scott had asked you to command the northern armies.

Lee: I don't know who could have heard that. Not that there's any secret about it.

His Partner: Oh, I shouldn't be asking questions, I know. But every mooring seems suddenly to have broken.

Lee: I know. The Potomac there is so peaceful, isn't it? All my life it has seemed so friendly, looking at it from north or south. And now, for both shores, what is coming?

His Partner : They oughtn't to have done it.

Lee : It's gone beyond that now. There's nothing left for each of us now but the last decision, and then to forget that it ought not to have been done, that somebody was foolish. We shall all have to believe that we are wise and just. That's the way of these things. Argument is over, and faith begins.

His Partner : But faith in what ? Massachusetts shall we say, or Virginia ?

Lee : Faith that we have chosen well.

His Partner : For the man there, and the man here ?

Lee : For both of them ; I would ask no less for either.

His Partner : And yet the decision is troubling you.

Lee : Very little now. A life's work, a devotion, some credit by good fortune—it takes a moment to put all these aside, but hardly longer.

His Partner : Even though, as I have heard you say, you don't altogether agree with Virginian policy ?

Lee : To-morrow I shall have forgotten that Virginia has a policy, and remember only that she is Virginia.

His Partner : That's how John loves Massachusetts, I know it. What are we to do ? You see, I'm Virginian too.

Lee : You must go with him—if you think you must. Did Mrs. Lee thank you for the bacon ?

His Partner : Yes—I'm glad you like it.

Lee : We can't seem to manage it here just like that, somehow. How far did you get, Tom ?

Buchanan : Only to Whitewater Woods, sir. That kept us busy.

Lee : You said you wanted to speak to me. Is it something private ?

Buchanan : Well no, Colonel Lee, it's not that. Of course, we're all thinking about the same thing. Would you mind if I fetched David and Ray ?

Lee : Certainly not.

> BUCHANAN *goes.* LEE *opens the door on to the verandah.*

Lee : It's quite warm. Spring is forward this year. Do you mind the door being open, ladies ?

His Partner : No, Colonel.

Elizabeth : I'm sure we could all do with a little air, Colonel Lee. I suppose there has got to be fighting ?

Lee : I'm afraid so, Betty. A lot of it.

Elizabeth : Tom and I were to be married next month.

Lee : I shouldn't put it off.

Elizabeth : But—mightn't it be worse for him ?

Lee : You're a dear girl, Betty. Of course not. Very much better for him, whatever happens.

BUCHANAN *returns, with* PEEL *and* WARRENTON.

Lee : Well ? Another kind of convention, eh ?

Buchanan : You see, sir, we may not get a chance of speaking to you again like this. We don't know what you're going to do, and it's not for us to ask. But there's certain to be a call for volunteers to-morrow, I suppose, sir ?

Lee : I expect so.

Buchanan: Then David and Ray and Duff and I are going to join.

Duff: Yes, we're all for soldiers, sir.

Lee: Well?

Buchanan: And if you are on Virginia's side sir——

Lee: If I am on Virginia's side?

Buchanan: I beg your pardon, sir. I mean——

Peel: It wasn't for us to assume what you were going to do, sir.

Lee: All right, Tom, only—— It's no matter. What is it?

Buchanan: We want to serve together, and we hoped that it might be possible for you to let us do it under you, sir.

Elizabeth: Do let them, Colonel Lee.

Warrenton: I know my father would be awfully pleased if you said yes, sir.

Lee: He's a very old friend of mine, Ray. Very well, Tom, I'll do what I can, I promise.

Buchanan: Thank you, sir.

Penner: Do you think, sir, I could be allowed to take a small matter of a banjo with me?

Lee: I shouldn't ask that officially if I were you, Duff.

Penner: I see, sir. Just a private banjo.

Lee: Keep in touch with me, all of you.

Peel: We will, sir.

JOHN STEAN *comes back.*

Stean (*to his wife*): We must be going, my dear. It takes a good hour.

3

Mrs. Stean (rising): Yes, John. Thank you so much, Colonel Lee.

> *She shakes hands with him, and the rest.*

Lee (to STEAN): I'm very sorry about your difficulties, Mr. Stean.

Stean: And I for yours, Colonel. Thank you. I've many good friends in Virginia. And Lucy. It's very hard.

Lee: I hope we shall all be good friends again yet.

Stean: Good-night, Colonel.

> *He shakes hands, and goes with* MRS. STEAN, *their voices coming from the next room.*

'Good-night, Mrs. Lee . . . Good-night, Mrs. Lee.'

> DUFF *and his partner follow.*

Elizabeth: Will you take me, Tom? I must be going too.

Buchanan: Yes, my dear.

Elizabeth (shaking hands with LEE): You are quite sure about next month ?

Lee: Quite.

Elizabeth: Thank you.

Buchanan: Good-night, sir.

Lee: Good-night, Tom.

> BUCHANAN *and* ELIZABETH *go.*

Warrenton: I expect my people will be ready. Good-night, sir.

Lee: Good-night, Ray.

> WARRENTON *goes.*

Peel: Might I speak to you, Colonel Lee ?

Lee: Why, certainly.

Peel: It's no good pretending it's just a guest and

his host now.   It's Colonel Lee and one of thousands
of young Virginians.   You haven't answered Washington yet, sir, but we all know well enough what the
answer will be.   And I'm going to join the army to-
morrow—to fight against—whom ?—the fellows just
the other side of the Potomac there.   So that's all
settled.   But will you answer a question, sir ?

Lee : If I can.

Peel : Are you happy about Virginia, sir ?

Lee : David, my boy, I was bred and have lived as
a soldier.   I think the politicians are often foolish
enough, and stubborn too.   But you've got to leave
these things to them.   If they make mistakes, so
should we.   Whichever way the decision had gone
there would have been some misgiving.

Peel : I can't help feeling that the quarrel, whatever it is, is so little beside the desolation that's
coming.

Lee : I know.   But everybody feels that really.
The trouble is that the world goes on without caring
for our feelings.   Only an odd adventurer here and
there really wants wars.   But the strain comes, and
men's wits break under it, and fighting is the only
way out.   A weak way, but the only one.

Peel : But if everyone had sense——

Lee : Everyone has—up to the strain at breaking-
point.   War is the anger of bewildered peoples in
front of questions that they can't answer.   But these
questions that they can't answer will come, and the
anger will come too.   I loathe war—I've seen too
much of it.   But I've never regretted being a soldier.

Peel: Then you do think that they may be as right as we are—or we as wrong as they?

Lee: Robert Lee may think it. But Virginia cannot and must not think it. And Robert Lee is now part of Virginia. You aren't David Peel any longer— you are a part of a people that cannot answer a question. You may be wiser than Virginia, but your wisdom doesn't matter till she doesn't need you any more in her quarrel. I can see it in no other way.

Peel: You mean that you, or any of us, may be wiser than the state, and yet the state is the great good for which we must give all, life perhaps?

Lee: A tragic mystery. But inescapable. And a mystery not without beauty, strangely not without it.

Peel: I think I see a little.

Lee: It all tells us not to put too high a value on life—or, rather, a wrong one. If to go on living were the only possible good, it would be different.

Peel: Then—but it would be impertinent.

Lee: No—ask anything.

Peel: Everybody knows about your seeing General Scott this morning. Why did you feel you couldn't give your answer then?

Lee: Because the habit of thirty years is difficult to throw off in a moment. I wanted to keep an open mind for a few hours if possible, for any consideration to come in that might. So much depended on the answer. But I had little doubt as to what it would be. I prepared General Scott for it.

Peel: Thank you. I know what you are giving up.

Lee: Whatever we give up, David, we keep something that we want more.

> *The music starts again.*

Lee: That's the last dance. I know they will very kindly excuse me. But go and do your duty, David.

Peel (shaking hands): Good-night, sir.

> *He goes.*

> LEE *looks out for a moment across the river. Then he goes out by a door on the other side of the room.*

> PENNER *and* PEEL *and their partners, and one or two other dancing couples come in and out of the room. While it is empty for a moment* LEE *comes back, wearing an overcoat, and goes out on to the verandah, where he is seen walking up and down. The dancing goes on.*

> *Again the room is empty, and a* SERVANT *comes in from the door that* LEE *last used. He looks round, discovers* LEE, *and goes to him.*

Servant: Major Perrin has come from Washington to see you, sir.

Lee: Major Perrin?

Servant: Yes, sir.

Lee: Bring him in here.

Servant: Yes, sir.

> *He goes.*

> LEE *goes to the dancing-room, and speaks at the door.*

Lee: Do you mind if I close this door, my dear? There's a message from Washington.

Mrs. Lee's voice: Certainly.

He closes the door. The music is still heard beyond it. LEE *takes off his overcoat, and closes the verandah door. The* SERVANT *shows* PERRIN *in.*

Lee : Good-evening, Major.

Perrin : Good-evening, sir. This is from General Scott.

Lee (*taking letter*): Sit down, will you ?

PERRIN *sits, while* LEE *reads. The* SERVANT *brings in a drink on a tray, which* PERRIN *takes. The* SERVANT *goes.*

Lee : Are you going back to-night ?

Perrin : Yes, sir. My boat is waiting.

Lee : There seems to be some haste.

Perrin : I understand that Mr. Lincoln wished it.

Lee : My letter is not yet written.

Perrin : General Scott authorised me to take a message, the letter to follow.

Lee : So he tells me. There was nothing else (*indicating the letter*) ?

Perrin : The General asked me to say informally that the army commanders to whom he has spoken to-day welcome the suggestion that you should be given control.

Lee : They are very considerate. But there's no belief that I shall come ?

Perrin : I can't say that, sir. I think everybody has great faith in your loyalty.

Lee : I, too, have faith in that.

Perrin : Its not for me to say anything more, sir.

Lee : My compliments to General Scott. My resignation will be in his hands by to-morrow at noon.

Perrin (rising) : Yes, sir.

Lee (ringing a bell) : Can I be of any assistance to you ?

Perrin : Thank you, no, sir.

> *The* SERVANT *comes.*

Lee : See that Major Perrin is conducted to his boat.

Servant : Yes, sir.

> *He goes with* PERRIN.

> LEE *puts on his overcoat again. After a pause, he opens the dance-room door, and looks in for a moment. Then he goes out again on to the verandah. As he walks up and down the* SERVANT *comes, and puts out the lantern lights, leaving the clear night sky beyond. After a few moments the music stops and* DUFF PENNER *comes in from the dance-room. He hesitates, until he sees* LEE *passing on the verandah. As* LEE *comes back to the door he speaks.*

Penner : Oh, we're just going. Good-night, Colonel Lee.

Lee (at the verandah door) : Good-night, Duff. But it's not Colonel Lee any longer.

Penner : Not Colonel—— (*He stands for a moment, then turns back to the dance-room excitedly, and begins to speak to the people beyond.*) I say—— (*He checks himself. Then after a moment he goes up to* LEE, *and holds out his hand.*) Will you let me, sir ? (*As* LEE *takes his hand.*) Lee of Virginia. (*He turns hurriedly and goes.*)

Lee (after a pause, not moving) : Virginia.

THE SCENE CLOSES.

SCENE IV.

Twilight on the evening of June 30th, 1862. The eve of the action at Malvern Hill, which closed the seven days' battle before Richmond.

At the approach to the hill, just outside the tent of GENERAL J. E. B. STUART, *the Commander of the Confederate cavalry.*

To and fro from the tent at intervals passes TOM BUCHANAN, *on sentry duty.* RAY WARRENTON, *his hat off and his uniform coat open, lies asleep on the ground.* DUFF PENNER, *coatless, smoking a cigar, his banjo across his knees, is sitting close by him, his back against a hummock of turf. On a flat piece of rising ground a few yards away,* DAVID PEEL *is lying at full length on his stomach, rifle in hand, watching the distance. For a few moments there is silence, but for* BUCHANAN'S *movement.*

Penner : Ray.

There is no answer.

Penner : Private Warrenton.

Still none.

Penner : Um. Nice sociable party this is. (*A pause.*) Anybody else tried to walk across the gap, David?

Peel : You'll hear about it if they do. Don't talk.

Penner : I'm very much obliged, I'm sure. Have another cigar, Duff? Thank you, Duff; I will. (*He takes one from his pocket and lights it.*)

BUCHANAN *passes again.*

I say, look here, Tom——

BUCHANAN *takes no notice and passes on.*

Don't speak to the sentry—quite so. Thank you.

Laughter comes from STUART'S *tent.*

Penner: Now why doesn't the General ask me to oblige him with another tune? Jeb Stuart knows what's what about a banjo, I can tell you, David.

Peel: Don't talk.

Penner: There isn't much encouragement to, is there? I do think that after five days of it we might sit down together and be a bit easy. We might all be dead.

Peel: You will be directly if you don't stop talking.

Penner: We probably shall be to-morrow, anyway. That's a nice sort of a hill to go and assault, that is. If I were General Lee——

Peel: Well, you aren't. Be quiet.

Penner: No. Not General Lee. Be quiet, Duff. Finish mending your coat, Duff. Have a nice party all by yourself, Duff. (*He takes up his coat, and continues a sewing operation already begun.*)

BUCHANAN *passes again.*

Penner: Mending my coat, Tom.

BUCHANAN *takes no notice, and goes.*

Mending my coat, Duff. (*He goes on sewing for a few moments.*)

Then the report of PEEL'S *rifle rings out.* PENNER *starts violently, stabbing his finger with the needle.* WARRENTON *turns over in his sleep.*

Penner: Oh, damn! Why didn't you tell me?

Peel (*attending to his rifle*): I wasn't thinking of you.

Penner: Nobody is thinking of me. What happened?

Peel : That's the third.

Penner : Three out of three.

Peel : Nice occupation for a fine June evening, isn't it ?

Penner : Well, they should go to bed.

Peel : To bed. Yes.

Penner : It is pretty bloody.

Peel : Just. (*He resumes his vigil.*)

Penner (*biting off the cotton and inspecting his work*) : Four good marks, privately awarded by myself.

WARRENTON *wakes up.*

Penner (*putting on his coat*) : Good-evening.

Warrenton : I've been to sleep.

Penner : For three hours.

Warrenton (*rubbing his eyes*) : Where are we ?

Penner : Approaching Malvern Hill. Very unhealthy neighbourhood. Change here for death or glory.

Warrenton : I remember.

BUCHANAN *passes.*

I say, Duff, old man, that was a devil of a mess. Only this morning. It seems a year ago. I should never have got out if you hadn't turned up.

Peel (*over his shoulder*) : He's to be promoted for it.

Warrenton : I'm so glad. You were splendid.

Penner : I'll take your word for it. I don't remember it myself.

Again there is laughter from STUART'S *tent.*

Warrenton : That's a good laugh after fourteen months of this sort of thing.

Penner : Old Jeb will laugh at his funeral.

Warrenton : Not so old. They say he's only thirty.

Penner : Well, he knows enough to be older.

Warrenton: Have you heard anything about to-morrow?

Penner : General Jackson is expected here in the morning.

Warrenton : Stonewall. Then we shall do it.

Penner : Tom said there was something about General Lee coming here to see old Jeb to-night.

Warrenton : He finds time to do everything.

Penner : I know. I wonder he doesn't send for old Jeb to go to him. If I were——

Peel : As I said——

Penner : Quite right, I'm not.

> *The laughter comes out of the tent, and in a moment* GENERAL STUART, *familiarly Jeb, comes in accompanied by an* AIDE. STUART *is a young, heavily bearded man, splendid in looks and physique, sanguine and alive with a gay energy. He is at the moment in undress uniform, smoking a cigar, but marked with all the expansive elegance of the plumed and heavily spurred cavalier of the battlefield. He is the young cavalry leader loved by* LEE, *and probably the only man in the army who dares chaff* JACKSON.

Stuart (*to the* AIDE) : Wait for the General at New-ington cross-roads. He may be there at any time now.

The Aide (*going*) : Yes, sir.

Stuart (*to* WARRENTON, *who, with* PENNER, *is now standing*) : Well, Warrenton, none the worse for this morning?

Warrenton : No, sir, thank you.

Stuart : It was Penner here that got you out of that.

Warrenton : I know, sir.

Stuart : We shall hear more about it. A little promotion for the banjo.

BUCHANAN *passes.*

Penner : That's very good of you, sir. But might I say something ?

Stuart : Yes, what is it ?

Penner : Promotion won't mean being moved, will it, sir ? You see, we four have been with you like this for six months now, and that's better than commissions and all that sort of thing. We like being just outside your tent, so to speak, sir. It makes us feel like unofficial generals, if you understand, sir.

Stuart : You're good fellows. I don't want to lose any of you. I'll see to it, don't worry.

Penner : Thank you, sir. I should like just to forget about the promotion.

Stuart : What's been going on, Peel ?

Peel (still on the look out) : Two more since I saw you, sir.

Stuart : That ought to discourage them. You're a very special sort of a cavalryman, David.

As he speaks, the rifle goes again.

Stuart (turning) : Again ?

Peel : Yes, sir.

Stuart : That should settle it. Let us have the banjo, Penner, while we're waiting. Not too loud, perhaps.

Penner : I'm much obliged to you, sir.

While STUART *walks to and fro, puffing his cigar,* PENNER *plays and sings.*

Nelly Bly!   Nelly Bly!
  Bring de broom along.
We'll sweep de kitchen clean, my dear,
  And hab a little song.
Poke de wood, my lady lub,
  And make de fire burn;
And while I take my banjo down,
  Just give de mush a turn.
      (*Chorus*) Heigh! Nelly, ho! Nelly,
              Listen, lub, to me,
              I'll sing to you, play to you
              A dulcem melody.

Nelly Bly shuts her eye
  When she goes to sleep.
And when she wakens up again
  Her eyeballs 'gin to peep.
De way she walks, she lifts her foot,
  And den she puts it down,
And when it falls dere's music dar
  In dat part of de town.
      (*Chorus*) Heigh! Nelly, ho! Nelly,
              Listen, lub, to me,
              I'll sing to you, play to you
              A dulcem melody.

Stuart: Very good, very good.   ' In dat part of de town.'   So there is.   Bless them.   I should like to make General Jackson sing that.

Penner: Any time you wish, sir.

> *During the song* BUCHANAN, *now off duty, has
> joined the party, smoking a cigar.   Another
> sentry has taken his place.   Night has now fallen,
> and they are in moonlight.   The glow of the fire
> comes from the direction of* STUART'S *tent.*

Stuart : The General didn't say any definite time,
Buchanan ?

Buchanan : About nightfall, sir, that was all.

Stuart (*humming to himself*) :

> And when it falls dere's music dar
>
>   In dat part of de town.

Penner (*offering to play*) : Would you like it again,
sir ?

Stuart : No thank you—here's the General coming.
(*He goes to his tent.*)

Buchanan : Well, Duff, what about bed ?

Penner : Bed, did you say ?   What's that ?

Buchanan : Sleep, then.   We shan't be wanted
again to-night.

Warrenton : But if we stay perhaps General Lee
will speak to us.

Penner : I'm sure I shall be very glad for anyone
to speak to me.   You're an agreeable sentry, Tom,
aren't you ?

Peel : Duff has become very well acquainted with
himself this evening.

Penner : And he's better company than some.

> LEE, *now Commander-in-Chief of the Army of
> Northern Virginia, comes in with* STUART'S AIDE
> *and his own.   He wears a light cloak.   At the
> same moment* STUART *returns, having put on his*

hat—very broad-brimmed with a large black plume—and his sword-belt.

Stuart: Good-evening, sir.

Lee: Good-evening, General.

Stuart: This way, sir.

Lee: I would rather stay outside. It's very hot to-night.

Stuart: Yes, sir.

Lee (*spreading his cloak on the ground, and sitting*): You've still got your young men, I see. Good-evening, Ray.

Warrenton: Good-evening, sir.

Lee: How's the banjo, Duff?

Penner: The General is being very kind to it, sir.

Lee: Oh, Tom, you took my pencil away this afternoon.

Buchanan: Did I, sir (*feeling in his pocket*)? So I did. I'm extremely sorry, sir. (*Gives it to* LEE.)

Lee: It's all right. Only my own staff will never let me keep one. They collect them, I imagine.

Lee's Aide: I'll speak about it, sir.

Stuart: Good-night. I shan't want you again. Four o'clock in the morning.

BUCHANAN, PENNER, *and* WARRENTON *go, with 'Good-night, sir. Good-night, sir.'*

Stuart (*to the* AIDES): You'll find some excellent peaches in the tent, gentlemen.

The AIDES *go.*

Lee: Sit down, General.

Stuart: Thank you, sir. (*He sits beside* LEE.)

Lee: Smoke if you want to.

Stuart : Thank you, sir. I do find it helpful. (*He lights a cigar.*) By the way, sir, I suppose we can count David Peel there as deaf ?

Lee : Hullo, David.

Peel : Good-evening, sir.

Lee : What's he doing ?

Stuart : They've been sending scouts across from Taylor's Farm all the evening, trying to see what's happening on our left. There's just one point where they miss cover. Peel's been watching it.

Lee : I see. We can leave him to it.

Stuart : Why didn't you send for me, sir ?

Lee : No—I wanted a walk. About to-morrow.

Stuart : Yes, sir.

Lee : Those people have a very strong position. We've driven them for a week, but there they are. They grow as you kill them. To take that hill to-morrow will be to send our men through hell. But we shall get there. The question is whether we can destroy them. In any case we've saved Richmond— for a time. Is it for more than a time ? That depends on to-morrow.

Stuart : We must destroy them. What am I to do, sir ?

Lee : You may not be there.

The Sentry passes.

Stuart : Not there, sir—but——

Lee : No. That's what I wanted to see you myself for. We depend more than anything else on having Jackson with us.

Stuart : Well, sir ?

Penner : What is it ?

Peel : I don't know.

Penner : People never want to talk at the right time, and they always want to talk at the wrong time.   I was fast asleep.

Peel : You're lucky.

LEE *with his* AIDE *returns with* STUART.

Lee : Very well, then.   Report to me at the first possible moment.   Good-night.   Good-night.

Stuart : Good-night, sir.

Peel and Penner : Good-night, sir.

LEE *and his* AIDE *go.*

Stuart (*to Penner*): I want you and Warrenton to fetch Colonel Wright and Major Trelawny here at once.

Penner : Yes, sir.

STUART *returns to his tent.*

Penner : That's one for Ray, anyhow.   Look here, David, what's it all about ?

Peel : Don't ask me.   But do you remember that day in the woods at Arlington ?

Penner : I do.

Peel : Well, I told Tom and Ray then.

Penner : What ?

Peel : This.

Penner : How, this ?

Peel : We've won battles for a year.   We've won them every day for a week.   We've beaten them and beaten them.   And there they are.

Penner : There they are, certainly.

Peel : And they'll be there longer than we shall. That's all.

Penner : I say—you give me the shivers.

Peel : But we shall be a wonder of the world yet. Perhaps in the end we shall have only one thing left.

Penner : What's that ?

Peel : Robert E. Lee.

Penner : Perhaps. . . . I say, Ray . . . (*calling*). (*He goes.*)

> PEEL *lifts his rifle, holds it at aim for a moment, then lowers it again without firing, and continues to watch.*

THE SCENE CLOSES.

SCENE V.

Early evening of the next day, July 1st, 1862.

An open space from which could be seen the action on Malvern Hill, which has been in progress some three hours. The sound of firing is continuous.

LEE *is watching the action. With him is his* AIDE.

Lee (after a prolonged scrutiny of the field) : Hill can't go on doing that for ever. Go to Captain Parkes again—ask him if there's any news of General Jackson's advance yet.

The Aide : Yes, sir.

He goes.

After a moment TOM BUCHANAN *comes on.*

Buchanan (saluting) : General Stuart is ready, sir.

Lee : Yes, I know, but we aren't. We can't move them, yet. Tell General Stuart to keep as near Long Spinney as he can with safety, and wait. He may have to wait most of the night.

Buchanan (going) : Yes, sir.

Lee : Any news of Betty ?

Buchanan : Yes, sir. I've got a son.

Lee : Splendid. Give her my love.

Buchanan : Thank you, sir.

He goes. The AIDE *returns.*

The Aide : General Jackson is moving, sir. He expects to be in action within half an hour. He is coming up across us here.

Lee : Good. Now go down to Colonel Cooper. Tell him to take the Sixteenth and the Forty-Ninth up to support Magruder's right at once.   And let the Tenth and Fourteenth be ready to follow.

The Aide: Yes, sir.   Won't you eat something, sir?

Lee: Oh, yes, thank you.   I had forgotten.

> *The* AIDE *goes, and* LEE *takes a small piece of bread and an apple from his pocket, and eats them.   He walks up and down, eagerly watching the action.   Then he takes another apple from his pocket.*

Lee: Have an apple, Mason.

> *He throws it to a man a few yards away.*

A Voice: Thank you, sir.

> *Still* LEE *moves about, then, suddenly—*

Lee: No, no, no.   Come here, Mason.

> CAPTAIN MASON *comes on.*

Mason: Yes, sir.

Lee: Go along to Hurd's battery as quickly as you can.   Tell them they must keep to the right of those trees, or they'll cut into Hill's advance.   I warned them about it.   Quickly.

Mason: Yes, sir.   You ought to find some cover, sir.   It's not safe here.

Lee: Go along, Mason, do as you are told.   It's perfectly safe.

Mason: Yes, sir.

> *He turns to go, and falls dead at* LEE'S *feet, shot through the heart.*

Lee (*kneeling over him*): Poor lad, poor lad.

> *Another officer,* CAPTAIN UDALL, *runs on, and kneels beside him.*

Udall: He's dead.   You must not stay here, sir.

Lee : Go down to Hurd's battery immediately. Tell them that if they don't keep their fire to the right of those trees they'll cut up Hill's advance.

Udall : Yes, sir. Do move, sir. We're just getting them—it would be disastrous if anything happened——

Lee : Hurd's battery, Udall, at once. I'll move Mason.

Udall : Yes, sir.

> *He goes.*
>
> LEE *lifts* MASON'S *dead body, and is about to carry it off, when* BUCHANAN *returns.*

Buchanan : What is it, sir ?

Lee : Mason, poor fellow, killed.

Buchanan : Let me move him, sir.

> LEE *puts down the body, and* BUCHANAN *kneels by it.*

Buchanan : General Stuart wants to know whether it would be possible for you to speak to him, sir.

Lee : How far is it ?

Buchanan : A four-minutes' gallop, sir.

Lee : Very well.

Buchanan : I'll put him under that tree. You shouldn't expose yourself like this, sir.

Lee : Look here, Tom, that's three of you. One would think this army's business was to look after me. It's mine to look after it, and myself.

Buchanan : But you can't look after it if you get shot, sir.

Lee : Don't argue. See to Mason, and then show me the way.

Buchanan: Yes, sir.

> *He carries* MASON's *body off.*
>
> *The* AIDE *returns.*

The Aide: Colonel Cooper is moving into action now, sir. Major Hurd says he has your message. Captain Udall was killed as he gave it.

Lee: Udall, too. Bring the horses—I'm going to see General Stuart. Come with me.

The Aide: Yes, sir.

> *He goes.*
>
> BUCHANAN *returns.*

Buchanan: I think General Jackson is moving by here directly, sir.

> *His arm falls, broken by a shot.*

Lee (*supporting him*): Tom, my boy.

Buchanan: It's nothing, sir, really nothing. This way, sir.

> *He moves to go. A rifle shot is heard a few yards away, and a moment after* DAVID PEEL *comes on, rifle in hand, looking into the distance.*

Peel: It's just one man, sir. I've been watching his smoke for an hour. He won't do any more.

Lee: Tom is hit, David. Fetch a doctor, there's one just along there.

Buchanan: It isn't anything at all, sir.

Peel: Hurt, old man?

Buchanan: No, David, nothing at all. Shall we go, sir?

> *He faints.* PEEL *catches him. He attends to him with a flask.*

Lee: I'll look after him. Fetch the doctor.

Buchanan (*coming to*): It's all right, sir.

Peel: I'll take him along, sir.

> *He helps* BUCHANAN *off.*
> LEE *watches the action again.*

Lee: That's better. (*As though giving orders*) Keep it to the right—that's it—that's it.

> *The* AIDE *comes in.*

The Aide: The horses are ready, sir. General Jackson is just coming up the path.

Lee: What, by himself?

The Aide: I think so, sir. One of General Ewell's brigades is passing along the road under us. I saw General Jackson dismount, and leave the road by himself.

> PEEL *returns.*

Lee: Where's Tom?

Peel: The doctor is looking after him, sir. A broken arm, but not serious.

Lee: Go back to General Stuart, will you? Say that I was coming, but that General Jackson is here, and if he can possibly come up to see me, will he do so? If not, I will be with him in half an hour.

Peel: Yes, sir.

> *He goes.*

Lee: What's that moving down there, by the barn.

The Aide: I think it's Hurd's battery moving forward, sir.

Lee: That's it. That means that McClellan is moving too. He'll be in retreat before dark, but he's going to get away, he's going to get away.

The Aide: But Richmond is safe, sir.

Lee: If we could have destroyed him. . . . Did you take my message to General Whiting this morning about Denison?

The Aide: Yes, sir.

Lee: What did he say?

The Aide: He said, all right, sir. But Major Denison, I gathered, had been heard to criticise you, sir.

Lee: It's not what he thinks of me, but what I think of him. Has he been put in command of Whiting's scouts?

The Aide: Yes, sir. General Whiting gave the order while I was there.

Lee: There go Ewell's men. If Hill can hold out for five minutes. It's a terrible place to cross. They're doing it—yes, yes. Now if Whiting can come in from the left.

The Aide: Here's General Jackson coming, sir.

GENERAL JACKSON, '*Stonewall*', *comes in, scanning the field as he walks. The fighting Puritan of the army, with ragged beard, and iron visionary eyes, he wears no arms, and has his hat in his hands behind him.*

Lee: General.

Jackson (putting his hat on and saluting): I didn't know you were here, sir.

Lee: You managed to get through.

Jackson: I was held up twenty times. But I got here, with the help of Stuart.

Lee: Ewell looks like getting up to Hill in a minute. Where's Whiting?

Jackson : I think he'll join Hill's left almost at once. I sent up one of my own brigades to him from reserve. There's just one gap—about two hundred yards. It begins just there—beyond that foot-bridge. I left Hewitt with the Third Carolinians to get across to it. If we fill that, Whiting and Hill will be in touch. But it's a bad place to get to.

Lee : I don't see any movement there.

Jackson : No. I don't like it.

Lee : If we can't destroy McClellan to-night, if he gets away, it means beginning all over again.

Jackson : I know, sir.

Lee : Ewell is right through now. What's happening to Hewitt ?

Jackson : I must go back and see for myself.

> COLONEL HEWITT, *covered with the marks of action, hatless and gripping the bladeless hilt of a sword, comes in. He salutes.*

Jackson : Hewitt ! What are you doing here, man ?

Hewitt : It's no good, sir. I can't get across. I've sent them twice, and led them twice. Every yard of the ground is swept.

Jackson : You must get across.

Lee : The whole line depends on it, Colonel.

Hewitt : Half my Carolinians are killed already.

Jackson : Get across with the other half. Don't stop, go on till there's not a man standing. That gap has got to be closed. There's no one else to close it.

Hewitt : It's annihilation, sir. Nothing can live there.

Jackson : Colonel, I always endeavour to take care of my wounded, and to bury my dead. You have heard my order—obey it.

Hewitt : Yes, sir.

He salutes and goes.

Lee : Hewitt is a good fellow.

Jackson : Not if he doesn't fill that gap, sir.

Lee : It's a beautiful line now—look at it. Magruder is well round on the right. Huger is touching Ewell—Hill—that little blank—Whiting.

Jackson : It shall be filled. (*He turns to go.*)

Lee : Where are you going?

Jackson : I'll take them across it myself.

Lee : You mustn't.

Jackson : I must, sir.

Lee : General Jackson!

Jackson : Very well, sir—but——

Lee : If any man can get them across, Hewitt can. To lose you would be to lose my right arm, Jackson. Go and do what you can—but not that. Promise me.

Jackson : All right, sir.

He goes.

Lee : That's clever of McClellan — look — he's moving men down to that gap. He'll cut Whiting off if Hewitt doesn't get over.

The Aide : I suppose there's no possible support to send Hewitt, sir?

Lee : None.

PEEL *returns.*

Peel : General Stuart will be here at once, sir.

Lee: You've got good eyes, David. Can you see past that foot-bridge?

Peel: Yes, sir. It's open. General Whiting is beyond it, I think, sir.

Lee: That is so. You see the enemy there moving towards the open place?

Peel: Yes, sir.

Lee: Is there anybody moving in front of them?

Peel (*after a moment*): Yes—a scout there in those trees—two, I think.

Lee: You can't reach them?

Peel: Not from here, sir.

Lee: Could you get near enough?

Peel: I'll try, sir.

Lee: Yes, do.

Peel *very cautiously starts off on his mission.*

The Aide: Even if Hewitt fails, McClellan is bound to retreat now, isn't he, sir?

Lee: Yes—but he could hold out then till it's dark, and he would get clear away to James's River.

General Stuart *arrives.*

Lee: Good-evening, General.

Stuart: Good-evening, sir.

Lee: You brought him through all right.

Stuart: Yes, sir.

Lee: It was very well done. You wanted to see me?

Stuart: Couldn't I move out beyond General Whiting now, sir? I'm sure I could drive their right in on to our centre.

Lee: That's just what you couldn't do, Jeb.

They've got earthworks on their right that would defeat all the cavalry in the world. I've seen them, and I know.

Stuart : You've seen them, sir ?

Lee : Yes, last night.

Stuart : You tell us to be careful, sir, and you set us a very bad example.

Lee: Well, you can't move until they do. We can't get round them, we've got to go through them, or after them.

Stuart : Of course, if you say so, sir. I'm tired of sitting and looking on. And they've put a bullet through Penner's banjo. That doesn't make things any more cheerful.

Lee : What's that happening there ?

The Aide: It's the Carolinians, sir. Hewitt is trying to get by on this side of the bridge. It's shorter, but it must be even worse.

Lee: He's splendid. He's going to do it.

Stuart : Look here, sir, I can't stand this. For God's sake, let me do something.

Lee: Wait here. I'll tell you when you can go.

JACKSON *comes back hurriedly.*

Jackson: You see, sir ?—Hewitt is almost through. Give me back my word, sir—I could get them over, I'm sure of it.

Lee: If you people don't be quiet, I'll put you under arrest. Leave Hewitt alone. (*To the* AIDE) Go to General Huger—tell him to drive their left back, round on Magruder if he can. Tell him not to mind getting out of touch with Ewell now—they can't spare any men from their centre to do any harm there. (*The* AIDE *goes.*) That's good—one more drive—I told you, Jackson.

Stuart : He hasn't more than a couple of hundred men left.

Jackson : They'll be enough to hold it if they get there.

Lee : He's through—— Oh! that's too bad.

Stuart : He's down.

Jackson : I must go, sir, I must. I told you. They'll break—they are breaking.

Lee : You could do no more than he has done.

Stuart : They are coming back—hardly a hundred of them.

Jackson : We must go again. I've still got my own Fifty-Third, sir. They're worn out, but they'll go with me. Let me take them, sir.

Lee : It's too late now—it will be dark in ten minutes. Somebody is fetching Hewitt. That's brave of him. No, Jackson, time has beaten us. If we could have attacked this morning we might have destroyed them in spite of all.

Jackson : I'm sorry, sir.

Lee : It wasn't your fault. If it had been in human power for you to have got here last night, you would have done it. I know that. We've beaten them, but they will get away—enough of them to give us no rest.—Look, though, they're retreating. Yes, surely—yes, from their centre to their left. Huger has driven their left in, and it's taken the centre with it. Now then, Jeb, boy, you can go. It's a clear road for you now—straight up the front slope. Do all you can.

Stuart : Yes, sir.

> *He goes, and is heard mounting and riding away.*

> *The* AIDE *returns.*

The Aide : General Huger was expecting your order, sir.

> BUCHANAN *comes in, his arm in a splint.*

Buchanan : I'm all right now, sir. Can you use me ?

Lee : No, Tom. Sit down and rest.

Buchanan : I really don't need it, sir.

Lee : Will nobody obey me ? Sit down.

Buchanan : Couldn't I go back to General Stuart, sir ?

Lee : General Stuart will be in pursuit of the enemy in a few minutes.

Buchanan : Then I really ought to be with him, sir.

Lee : Don't be foolish, and for the last time, sit down. I'll find something for you to do presently. The doctor should have kept you.

> BUCHANAN, *unconvinced, sits down on the ground and nurses his arm.*

Lee : Their right is moving back too.

Jackson : If Whiting knows, he can get in now. But he can't see through earthworks.

Lee (*to the* AIDE) : Ride for all you are worth—let Whiting know that he can get through.

The Aide (*going*) : Yes, sir.

Jackson : I'll go up myself, sir.

Lee : Yes, do. Report to me in the morning.

Jackson : Yes, sir.

> As JACKSON *is going, he meets* PEEL, *half-supporting and half-carrying* COLONEL HEWITT.

Peel : He insisted on being brought to you, sir. It's the lung, sir.

Hewitt : I'm sorry, General. I nearly did it. I—I——

Jackson : You were magnificent, Colonel. I had to send you.

Hewitt : I know, sir. I nearly did it. If they had—given—me—another—I nearly—tell General Lee——

> *He dies.*

Jackson (to LEE—*after a moment's pause)* : You're right, sir—I couldn't have done it as well.

> *He salutes and goes.*

Lee : David, you're a very gallant boy.

Peel : I got them both, sir. It kept the gap clear, I think. But there—it wasn't any use.

Lee : That's not for you to judge, David. But I meant bringing Colonel Hewitt in.

Peel : Anyone would have done that, sir.

> *The* AIDE *returns.*

The Aide : I was able to signal up, sir.

Lee : Very well. We'll move our quarters up the hill. See that bearers are sent for Colonel Hewitt. David, you had better follow General Stuart—he is advancing at once. Tom, stay with me. (*To the* AIDE) : Go and tell them—I want to walk along here a little way. I'll join you directly.

> *The* AIDE *goes in one direction,* LEE *in the other. It is now nearly dark. All the firing has ceased.*

5

Peel : For six months he has waited for this—and now——

Buchanan : They must have lost thousands, though, to-day.

Peel : There are thousands more to come. I must go.

Buchanan : I ought to come with you.

Peel : Of course you can't. I'm so glad about Betty.

Buchanan : Yes.

> PEEL *goes.*
>
> *A moment later the* AIDE *returns, carrying a lantern. He places it by* HEWITT'S *body.*

The Aide : Will you come with me? The General didn't wish us to wait.

Buchanan : Yes.

> *They go.*
>
> *A few moments later* LEE *comes back. Covering his face with his hand, for a little time he stands by* HEWITT'S *body. Then he takes off his cloak, and places it over the dead man. After a pause again,*

Lee (*speaking slowly*) : Have mercy upon us.

> *He follows* BUCHANAN *and the* AIDE.

THE SCENE CLOSES.

Scene VI.

The early evening of Sunday, May 10th, 1863.

The room of Jefferson Davis, *President of the Confederacy, at the Confederate White House, Richmond, Virginia.*

The window of the room is open to clusters of spring blossom. From the far distance comes the sound of church bells.

Jefferson Davis *is sitting at the table with a* Secretary.

Davis : General Lee is late.

Secretary : Hardly, Mr. President. He couldn't arrive in Richmond before five. It's only six now.

Davis : Yes, well—that will do. See that the Kentucky proclamation is sent off to-night. Did you ask whether there was any more news of General Jackson ?

Secretary : Nothing had come through this afternoon.

Davis : You are sure that General Lee got my letter before he started ?

Secretary : Yes, sir, Mason telegraphed that it had been delivered.

Davis : He knows I can't do it. I wish he wouldn't ask it.

Secretary (*deferentially*) : A great many people seem to think it is the right time, sir.

Davis: A great many people think a great deal

more than is good for them. Bring General Lee in directly he comes. And please tell Mrs. Davis that I shan't be able to go to church this evening.

> *The* SECRETARY *goes.* DAVIS *arranges some papers on his table, and then going to the window stands looking out. After a moment or two he calls to someone below.*

Davis : Are you better, Captain ?

A Voice : Yes, thank you, Mr. President. I'm going back to-morrow.

> DAVIS *waves a hand to him, and returns to his table, where he begins to write. The* SECRETARY *returns.*

Secretary (*at the door*) : General Lee, sir.

> LEE *comes in. The* SECRETARY *goes.*

Davis (*rising and shaking hands*) : Good-evening, General.

Lee : Good-evening, Mr. President.

Davis : Sit down, will you ?

> *They sit.*

Davis : You got my letter ?

Lee : Yes, Mr. President.

Davis : Yes, I'm glad you got it. I hope I was clear.

Lee : It is not for me to question your judgment. You are in a better position than I to see this matter clearly, I am sure. But I thought it necessary to tell you again just what I felt.

Davis : You are anxious, of course—we all are. But I suggest that anxiety may be indulged too freely.

Lee: As you will, Mr. President. I know very well that my place is to command the army in the field. But I cannot avoid thinking. How far, I must ask myself, will the resources of that army take us?

Davis: It has been suggested—by some, shall we say responsible, journals?—that you should be given entire control, both of the army and of policy.

Lee: You know very well that such proposals are foolish, and cause me nothing but distress. I am very sensible of the consideration that you give always to my views. I cannot ask, nor do I wish, for more than that. Further, I see very clearly that our troubles at all times have but one cause. If I had been able to secure the destruction of the enemy, we should now have no difficulties. I have not been able to do so. In the circumstances, if anyone should be removed, it should be the military commander.

Davis: I beg you will not say these things. Your successes are the pride and the only assurance of us all. Now again. Nothing has been so decisive as Chancellorsville.

Lee: Not decisive, Mr. President. We did well, I know, but it was not decisive. That is just it. We win battles, constantly, but we get no nearer to a decision. That is why I raised this question again. You can appear now at the head of a victorious army. It seems to me to be opportune.

Davis: As I told you in my letter, reunion with the North is to me unthinkable.

Lee: I know you feel that, Mr. President. Perhaps you would wish me to say no more?

Davis: No, no—please do not suggest that I am not open to argument—from the proper quarter. Say what you will.

Lee: It is only that. We have followed up a year's work, from our defence of Richmond, with Chancellorsville. We have never done better. Hooker is defeated. The North has probably never felt the strain so severely as it does at this moment. We might make proposals with great authority now.

Davis: The only proposal I will make is for unconditional peace. Will Mr. Lincoln accept that, do you suppose?

Lee: Might not the terms be discussed when the proposals in general have been made? It may well be that our lead would persuade them to do all that we asked.

Davis: So long as I am President of these Confederate States I will consent to nothing but a plain assertion from the first. Washington drove us out of the Union. Very well, we will stay out, on our own terms.

Lee: They, of course, do not admit that.

Davis: Do you think they need your advocacy, General Lee?

Lee: Mr. President——

Davis: No, no—I beg your pardon. Oh—I know you think I'm very short-sighted.

Lee: Indeed, I think nothing of the sort. I desire exactly what you desire. But I must consider the possibilities of getting it. If I did not advise you from my knowledge of the army, I should fail in my duty.

Davis: But the army isn't going to fall to pieces, is it ?

Lee: Supplies have already begun to be very irregular.

Davis: What is the good of telling me that—I'm doing everything I can.

Lee: But the people as a whole are not doing everything they can. I don't think you can insist upon that too often or too strongly, Mr. President. We have been through more than two years now. Last winter, even, we had none too much of clothes or food. In less than six months winter will be here again. The north grows stronger every week. Do we?

Davis: I tell you, I won't accept the only terms that I know they would give—reunion.

Lee: Very well, sir. We must go on.

Davis: Is General Jackson's condition serious?

Lee: I'm afraid he will be off duty for a long time. I could have spared any man better.

Davis (*his mind fixed on the one subject*): Why, only yesterday I had a report from one of our men at Washington. Mr. Lincoln had been heard to say when he was told of Chancellorsville, that it made no difference—unconditional surrender was all that he would listen to now or at any time. You'll find that he will declare for Abolition directly. He's stubborn.

Lee: Isn't that all the more reason——

Davis: No. We're stubborn too.

A knock at the door.

Davis: Yes?

The SECRETARY *comes in.*

Secretary: A telegram for General Lee. (*He gives it to him and goes.*)

Lee (*reading*): Oh—no, no.

Davis: What is it?

Lee: Jackson is dying. No, no, he can't.

Davis (*taking the telegram*): I didn't know it was that.

Lee: But they said all danger was gone. It was just an arm. He can't be dying—he can't. My man Jackson.

Davis: Where is he?

Lee: By Guinea Station, below Spottsylvania. It's four hours away. I—I should like to see him.

Davis: You would hardly get there to-night.

Lee: But I ought to go. Jackson—he mustn't, he mustn't.

Davis: It would be a heavy loss. Any recommendation you may make, General——

Lee: Recommendation—yes. We must go on. I understand.

Davis: And I ask you not to allow these political considerations to hamper you. We stand for the honour of the South. It can be vindicated only by our complete success, or our destruction.

Lee (*rising—his mind at Guinea Station*): For the honour of the South, Mr. President. I am not unmindful of it. It should have been my life. He is a better man than I, abler to serve you.

Davis (*rising*): He is a great man, and you are generous. But you alone could not be replaced, General.

Lee: You don't know Jackson, Mr. President, not as I do. I must go to him.

He moves to go. A knock again at the door.

Davis: Yes.

The SECRETARY *comes in.*

Secretary: Another telegram for General Lee, sir.

He gives it to LEE, *and goes.*

Lee (*reading*): He is dead. Good-night, Mr. President. I return in the morning. Your information as to my movements is clear?

Davis: Yes. Good-night, General. I'll do all that I can about supplies.

Lee: If you please. My men complain very little.

He goes.

The church bells are still ringing, and far off is heard a regiment marching to the tune of 'Dixie.'

DAVIS *stands still for a moment, then goes to the window and shuts it, returns to his table and resumes his writing.*

THE SCENE CLOSES.

Scene VII.

*Again a year later.   Six o'clock on the morning of May
     12th, 1864.*

A room in a small farmhouse, Lee's *Headquarters
     during the battles round Spottsylvania Court House.*

Lee's Aide—*of the Malvern Hill battle—and* Tom
     Buchanan, *now a Captain on Lee's staff, are
     sitting at a table, maps and papers before them.   On
     a wooden bench, roughly improvised as a bed,* Ray
     Warrenton *lies asleep, a bandage round his head.
     The men's uniforms are worn, and the room is bare,
     the door is off its hinges, there are signs of shattered
     crockery, and torn curtains droop over a broken
     window.*

The Aide: It means retreating.

Buchanan: I'm afraid so.

The Aide: If they can hold out at Richmond, the
General means to get down to Petersburg, I think.

Buchanan: We ought to be able to hold that, for a
time.

The Aide: For a time.

Buchanan: Grant must have lost over twenty
thousand men in the last week.   But it doesn't seem
to make any difference to him.

The Aide: The General is worn out.   Ought I to
wake him ?   He said two hours.

Buchanan: I should give him a few minutes longer.

Warrenton (*waking—rather dazed*): I say, this is
uncommonly good of you, Tom—Captain.

Buchanan: Feel rested, old man?

Warrenton: Oh, I'm all right. Funny thing, I've been dreaming about Stonewall Jackson.

Buchanan: It's a year and two days since he died.

Warrenton: I know. I dreamt about him, and a river—you remember, that was the last thing he said—'No, no, let us pass over the river, and rest under the shade of the trees.'

Buchanan: Yes, I remember.

Warrenton: Well, the river was there, and the trees too, and he was talking to somebody.

The Aide: You were probably thinking about him yesterday. You are tired.

Buchanan: Is your head hurting?

Warrenton: Not much.

The Aide: Try to sleep again. There'll be a bed for you presently. You had a rough day.

Warrenton: No—I mustn't go to sleep. General Lee may want me.

Buchanan: He won't want you to-day. You ought to sleep.

Warrenton: By Jove—I know now who it was that he was talking to. It was old Jeb. That's queer, isn't it? Old Jeb. Let me see—where is he?

Buchanan: He's gone down to Yellow Tavern with three brigades to keep Sheridan out of Richmond if he can.

Warrenton: Why aren't I with him?

The Aide: You had to get through to Stamford—you know. Do go to sleep, there's a good fellow.

Buchanan (*going to him and moving his pillow*):

Yes, Ray, do. The doctor says there's nothing to worry about. You'll be all right after a rest.

Warrenton: Yes, that's nothing. But old Jeb— under the trees—that's who it was with Stonewall.

He drops off asleep again.

BUCHANAN *goes back to his seat.*

The Aide: I think I had better tell the General.

He goes to a door leading to another room.

The Aide: Are you awake, sir?

Lee (*inside*): Yes, yes.

The Aide: It's half-past six, sir.

Lee: Oh, yes, thank you.

The AIDE *returns to his place, and a moment later* LEE *comes in. He is tired, rather ill.*

Lee: How is Warrenton?

Buchanan: Rather restless, sir. But I don't think it's anything serious. A little dazed still.

The Aide: Do you think he might use your bed for an hour or two, sir?

Lee: Of course—why didn't you suggest it before? I could have done very well here. It was careless of me.

Buchanan (*going to* WARRENTON): Ray—Ray.

Warrenton (*waking*): Yes—what is it?

Buchanan: There's a bed for you. You will be more comfortable.

Helped by BUCHANAN, WARRENTON *stands up. His clothes are ragged and threadbare, his boots worn and broken.*

Warrenton: I'm very sorry about that paper, General—I can't think how——

Lee: That's all right, my boy. You told me all I wanted to know.

Warrenton: I can't remember—you know the Warrentons always——

Lee: There's nothing to be troubled about at all, Ray. You must have a good sleep.

Warrenton: But that was a funny dream I had— it was old Jeb—— You must look after him, sir.

Buchanan: Come along, Ray, you must lie down.

Warrenton: It's very good of you to take so much trouble.

He goes out, BUCHANAN *supporting him.*

Lee: It was a terrible strain for him, poor fellow. It was fine of him. Everybody is fine. I wish we could do something more for him. Isn't there a little of that jelly left ?

The Aide: I'm afraid there's been none for a week, sir.

Lee: No.

BUCHANAN *returns.* LEE *sits at the table.*

Lee: Is there any word from General Stuart yet ?

Buchanan: No, sir, I asked ten minutes ago. The field wire still isn't working. I'm afraid it's cut.

The Aide: Thorpe went out with four men to see if they could trace it yesterday evening. They got a message through eight miles down, and that's the last we've heard of them.

Lee: One of Sheridan's pickets, eh ?

The Aide: I expect so, sir. I've sent out again this morning, but we've heard nothing.

Lee: Anything from Richmond ?

The Aide: They were all right an hour ago. They thought General Stuart had held Sheridan up. It had given them time, and they seemed hopeful.

Buchanan: Couldn't you rest for another hour or two, sir? General Grant won't be able to attack again until midday in any case. Everything you ordered has been done, sir. You really need it.

Lee: No, I must go and see Ewell before Grant strikes. It's too much to ask of him, too much. But it must be. How many men has he?

The Aide: Allowing for the loss of General Johnson's division, between eight and ten thousand all told, sir.

Lee: And Grant can use forty thousand at least there. It's more than any man can do.

Buchanan: I was talking to Pearson last night, sir. He says General Ewell is very troubled about it—the Johnson disaster is a great blow to him. He thinks he may be destroyed altogether to-day.

Lee: I know, I know. Petersburg is our only hope—siege—and then—— (*To the* AIDE) Write this to the President.

The AIDE *writes.* BUCHANAN *works at his papers.*

Lee (*dictating*): ' His Excellency President Davis. Mr. President, I have the honour again to bring to your notice the extremely precarious condition of our army in the field. Repeated assaults upon our lines by General Grant with a force at least twice as large as our own, has failed to break either the resistance or the determination of our men. But this cannot continue. Ewell, for example, who has been in

action for five days against a continually reinforced
enemy, will have this morning to meet a fresh attack
in which he will be outnumbered by four to one. I
have no men that I can move from any other part of
the line to help him. We have further to consider
that a strong Federal force is moving up the Valley
of Virginia under Hunter. We can there make no
opposition. In addition to Sheridan's threatened
raid upon Richmond, Butler with some thirty thousand troops is moving, almost as he will, in the same
direction. In the west Johnston's resistance to
Sherman is weakening daily, as it must do. And I
see no prospect of anything but increasing difficulty.
In the circumstances I must again press the advis-
ability of withdrawing our forces into the Petersburg
defences. We could hold out there for a considerable
time—long enough, I hope, to enable Your Excellency
to make what proposals you may think fit. But in
the open field I can no longer look for any favourable
results. I do not wish to call upon a devotion and
heroism, which have never been excelled, for one
moment after there has ceased to be a reasonable
hope of their being rewarded by victory in the end.
Unless, therefore, Your Excellency has some reason
which I have overlooked to urge against such a
course, I propose to withdraw this army to Petersburg as soon as I can do so. I have the honour to
be, with high respect, Your obedient servant . . .'
. . . I would have died rather than write it. There,
Tom, my boy, you see I have failed.

The AIDE *begins to transcribe the letter.*

Buchanan: You haven't, sir—not a man in the world will think it.   You have given our South a name for ever.

Lee: No—it is you—all of you—that have done that.   Virginia trusted me—they all did—and I was not good enough.   But there—I must not talk like this.   We must go on, right to the end.   Don't remember anything that I have said.   I must go now to Ewell.

> MRS. MEADOWS, *a hale but now hungry old housewife, comes in, carrying a tray with three cups of soup on it.*

Mrs. Meadows: It's thin, sir, but it's hot.

Lee: It's very kind of you, Mrs. Meadows.

Mrs. Meadows: It isn't kind at all, sir.

> LEE *takes his cup, and* BUCHANAN *and the* AIDE *theirs.   They drink, and* LEE *is about to do the same.*

Lee: There is a sick man in there, Mrs. Meadows. You must keep this for him.

Mrs. Meadows: Indeed no, sir—there's another cup.

Lee: And what are you having for breakfast yourself ?

Mrs. Meadows: There's plenty of breakfast for me, sir.   I never was much of a one for breakfast.

Lee (*placing his saucer on top of his cup*): Tom, take this to Warrenton, please.

Buchanan: Please, sir——

Lee: Now, now—I want to feel like a hero, you know.

{ *Buchanan* : But really, sir——
{ *Mrs. Meadows* : There is——
{ *The Aide* : I wish you would let——

Lee (*in humorous authority*) : Captain Buchanan.

Buchanan : Very well, sir.

> *He goes with* LEE'S *cup into the other room.*

Mrs. Meadows : But you must have some breakfast, sir.

Lee : Not every day.

Mrs. Meadows : You ought to have some to-day. You're not well, sir, anyone can see that.

Lee (*shepherding her away*) : I really don't need anything this morning.

Mrs. Meadows : There's an egg, sir, for your dinner.

Lee : Thank you.

Mrs. Meadows : You'll promise about that ?

Lee : Yes, when I come back.

> *She goes, pacified.* BUCHANAN *returns, and goes on with his work.*

Lee (*to the* AIDE) : Get that letter through at once. No, send it by telegraph. I should be back in an hour. I'll take Miller with me.

> *He is going; he is met at the door by* DAVID PEEL, *unshaven, his clothes derelict, and in a state of extreme exhaustion.*

Peel : Good-morning, sir.

Lee : David—what's this ?

Peel : The wire broke down at midnight, sir. They must have cut it. Our wire into Richmond was out of action, too, and they had cut our right off from the city itself. So they had to send me direct to you.

6

I left at one o'clock.   I should have been here before, sir, but I had to go round by Bampton to keep clear of them.

Lee: What's the news?

Peel: Good and bad, sir.   We've held General Sheridan up for three days.   I think Richmond can keep him out now.

Lee : Yes——

Peel: But General Stuart is killed, sir.

Lee: Stuart—— ?

Peel : Yes, sir—he's dead.   He was hit yesterday evening at Yellow Tavern.   He died at half-past twelve this morning.

Lee : Stuart—gone.   (*He pauses for a moment.*) You must rest, David.   (*To the others*) I'm going to Ewell.

   He goes out.   The AIDE *collects his papers and goes to send his telegram.*

Buchanan : Jeb Stuart.

Peel : He was magnificent, Tom.   Right in the thick of it all the time.—We implored him, but he wouldn't take any notice.   Tom, the end is coming.

Buchanan: Have you had any food?

Peel : I got my ration before I started.

Buchanan : I'm afraid we——

Peel : That's all right.   I'll see if I can sleep a little.

   He sits on the bench.

Buchanan : Did old Jeb suffer much?

Peel: He was unconscious most of the time.   All he asked for was Duff.

Buchanan : The banjo?

Peel : Yes.   What a man to love.

Buchanan : Do you remember that day before Richmond, two years ago ?

Peel : Yes.

Buchanan (*reconstructing with his finger*) : Out of the works, round to the back of them, and then clean through into Richmond again.

Peel : He's dead.

Buchanan : We've got to get into Petersburg.   Ray is in there—he's been badly shaken up.

Peel : Petersburg—and then.   Well, there's no more wondering.

WARRENTON *appears at the door.*

Warrenton : Hullo, David——

Buchanan : You must keep still, Ray——

Warrenton : No—I must find old Jeb—he's in danger—have you seen him, David ?

Peel : Yes, Ray, I've just come from Yellow Tavern.

Warrenton : You should have stayed to look after him. . . .   Oh, I see—he is really with Stonewall.

Buchanan : Do go and lie down, Ray.

Warrenton : Yes, I shan't see him any more.

He goes back.

Buchanan : There's nowhere to move him to yet.

Peel : The General seems worn out, too.

Buchanan : The greatest heart in the world, and it's pretty near breaking.

The AIDE *comes in.*

The Aide : What's to be done—word has just come

from Ewell that he has had to engage already. If the chief finds him in action nothing will keep him out of it—he's desperate.

Buchanan: I'll see if I can catch him—he wouldn't be going fast. He would probably come back to direct Rodes. As long as he doesn't get there and see it———

LEE *comes in hurriedly*.

Lee: General Ewell is in action—I picked the message up. Miller has gone on. Let General Rodes know that I want him to move in from the left to the centre in fifteen minutes' time. And send the Fourth and Ninth Batteries down to General Ewell's right at once. They must keep him from being cut off at any cost.

The Aide: Yes, sir.

The AIDE *goes*.

Lee: At any cost.

The AIDE *is heard speaking outside, and returns*.

The Aide: General Ewell is wounded, sir.

Lee: Take these orders. Captain Buchanan, come with me.

The Aide: Shall I find you here, sir?

Lee: Not for a time. I shall take over General Ewell's command myself. There is nothing more for me to do now.

Buchanan: But there is everything for you to do, sir. If we lost you———

Lee: Those orders, please.

The AIDE *goes*.

Lee: Come.

Peel: Please, sir, you mustn't, you mustn't. You let me speak to you that night at Arlington. Let me speak again, now. You mustn't go. It isn't brave to die now, sir. We all want to die in these days. The South is dying. There is nobody to save us but you. You must keep the South alive, sir, for the years to come. We all know we can't win now. But we haven't lost our courage. And we want you to use it, sir—not to die for it, but to live for it, so that when the end comes, we may be able to follow you still. To die would be to give in, sir.

Lee (pausing): You are right, David. We will go on to the end, together. Now go to sleep.

PEEL *lies down on the bench.*

Lee (to BUCHANAN): Let me see that map of the Petersburg road.

He sits as BUCHANAN, *standing beside him, places the map before him.*

Lee : Gordon must cover the withdrawal of the left and centre——

The AIDE *comes back.*

The Aide: I've sent your orders through, sir. General Ewell's wound is slight.

Lee : Let General Ewell know that I shall be there in twenty minutes.

The AIDE *goes.*

Lee (to PEEL, *who turns to him*): It's all right—I've promised. (*To* BUCHANAN, *at the map again*) It may be as much as ten days before we move. But in the meantime see that the roads east and west of Cold Harbor are . . .

THE SCENE CLOSES.

Scene VIII.

Jefferson Davis's *room at Richmond. An afternoon early in February,* 1865. *Outside is a white, frost-bound world.*

Davis—*a very tired man—and his* Secretary *are at the table.*

Secretary : I think that's all, sir.

Davis : Yes, that's all—all.

Secretary : We might bring it up to fifteen thousand in six weeks' time.

Davis : Fifteen—Grant alone has a hundred and twenty. We shall have to leave Richmond—they can't hold Petersburg long now.

Secretary : I'm afraid not, sir. I expect that is what Captain Buchanan is coming to say.

Davis : We must try to join General Johnston.

Secretary : General Lee will move to the West, I suppose.

Davis : I ought to have resigned six months ago.

Secretary : No, sir—nothing could have saved us. You have done all that could be done.

Davis : Thank you ; thank you. We have believed in what we did. And now, we shall be called outlaws.

Secretary : Mr. Lincoln will surely——

Davis : Mr. Lincoln will be merciful. Think of that—merciful. For four years we have laboured, and spent, and died, and Mr. Lincoln will be merciful. We should not have been made a proud people. Have the supplies from Kentucky come in ?

Secretary: I'm afraid they must have been cut off, sir.

Davis: We can expect nothing.   Take those papers to Mr. Farringdon.

> The SECRETARY *collects the papers and goes. For a few moments* DAVIS *sits at the table, his face covered by his hands.   Then the* SECRETARY *returns.*

Secretary: Captain Buchanan, sir.

> BUCHANAN *comes in.   He is from a broken army.   The* SECRETARY *sits at another table.*

Davis: You have brought a message from General Lee?

Buchanan: Yes, sir.

Davis: Sit down, please.

> BUCHANAN *does so.*

Davis: Well?

Buchanan: General Lee considers it necessary to abandon Petersburg to-morrow.   He proposes to move in the direction of Amelia Court House.

Davis: That means the surrender of Richmond.

Buchanan: Yes, sir.

Davis: The General thinks it imperative?

Buchanan: That or loss of the army, sir.

Davis: How did you get through?

Buchanan: I was lucky, sir.

Davis: To-morrow, you say?

Buchanan: Yes, sir.   General Lee wishes me to inform you of our condition.

Davis (shrinking): Yes, yes, I know.

Buchanan (as though reciting a message from memory): Our men have been in action since Sunday.   They have been without meat for three days—the worst days of this winter. They are suffering from reduced rations and scant clothing. Hail and sleet have been incessant. And the enemy's assaults go on day and night. General Lee has had to disperse his cavalry for want of forage. He fears that the physical strength of the men, even if their courage survives, must fail under this treatment. He wishes you to be prepared, sir, to hear of calamity at any time.

Davis: Can you get back to General Lee?

Buchanan: I think so, sir.

Davis: Tell him, I can do nothing.

Buchanan (*rising*): Yes, sir.

He moves to go.

Davis: Captain Buchanan.

Buchanan (*turning*): Yes, sir.

Davis: Tell him that. And say that I wish I could have served as nobly as he has done.

Buchanan: We worship him, sir. If it hadn't been for that, we couldn't have gone on.

Davis: I know. The South will always know.

Buchanan: But—you won't mind my saying it, sir?

Davis: What?

Buchanan: We all know what your burden has been, sir. General Lee has taught us that.

Davis: Good-bye.

Buchanan: Good-bye, sir.

He goes.

Davis (*after a pause, suddenly rising*): Send out every available officer, and telegraph wherever you can. Let supplies be bought or borrowed, or what you will, but let them be got. I won't let them starve, do you hear?

Secretary (moving to DAVIS's *table*) : We have tried every possible quarter, sir.

Davis: Say that General Lee and his men are starving, say that if we allow that we shall not only be defeated, we shall be disgraced.

Secretary : Everybody knows, sir—everybody has given, given. All the supplies left are beyond our reach. They can't be brought, and we can't fetch them.

Davis: They must be got, and more men must be raised——

Secretary : You have just seen all the papers, sir. Those are the facts.

Davis (quietly): Yes . . . the facts. Ask the members of the Cabinet to meet me here at five o'clock. This Government is at an end. We are going into exile.

> *The* SECRETARY *goes out, while* DAVIS *remains standing as*

THE SCENE CLOSES.

Scene IX.

Two months later. The line of Lee's *army in retreat, near Appomattox, April 9th,* 1865, *in the late afternoon. Outside* Lee's *tent.*

Propped against a heap of debris, Duff Penner *is lying with the remains of an overcoat covering him. On either side of him are seated* David Peel *and* Ray Warrenton. *All are in the last stages of fatigue and destitution.*

Warrenton : Any easier, Duff?

Penner : I don't feel it much now. Funny, on the last day. How long have I been here?

Peel : Over twenty-four hours. The doctor has just gone.

Penner : Whose tent is that?

Warrenton : General Lee's.

Peel : Don't you remember, he had you brought here?

Penner : So he did. It was kind of him. Did the doctor say anything about something to eat?

Peel : Presently.

Penner : Oh, of course—there isn't anything, is there?

Peel : There will be presently.

Penner : Yes, it's the last day, isn't it? Has General Lee gone?

Warrenton : They should be back soon. He's with Grant now.

Penner : Does the doctor think there's any chance?

Peel: Of course he does—you're going to get through all right.

Penner: Am I? Truth, you know.

Warrenton: We shall be able to move you this afternoon.

Penner: But will that help? I don't feel—am I going to die?

Warrenton: David told you no.

Penner: Yes, you did, David.

Peel: Really, Duff, old chap. It's missed the backbone all right. As soon as we can get you into proper quarters, you'll pull together in no time.

Penner: I'm a coward to worry about it. All the army is dying to-day really, isn't it?

Peel: It's coming to an end.

Penner: Yes, dying.

Peel: Beginning to live, perhaps.

Penner: Lee's army. Lee of Virginia.

Warrenton: I'm glad I've done that for the Warrentons.

Penner: Have you fellows been looking after me ever since I was hit?

Peel: We've just been watching you.

Penner: You're very good. I suppose the old banjo has gone.

Warrenton: I'm afraid so, Duff.

Penner: I'm sorry. Old Jeb gave it me, after the other one got smashed up. Aren't you fellows hungry?

Warrenton: David and I have discussed the matter for several hours, and have decided that we are not.

Penner : I suppose you don't know the terms of surrender ?

Peel : No, but a little food is about all we can hope for. And then we have got to build a world for ourselves.

Warrenton : Out of nothing.

Peel : Out of a memory. There are worse foundations.

Penner : It's very unfortunate about that banjo. It had a lot of memories. You know—— (*He sings softly*)

> I wish I was in the land of cotton,
> Cinnamon seed and sandy bottom.
> To the land, to the land, to the land, to the land;
> In Dixie's land where I was born,
> Early on one frosty morn.
> To the land, to the land, to the land, to the land;
> I wish I was in Dixie.

> *As he finishes some troops near by take up the song, and* PEEL *and* WARRENTON *join in. At the end* PENNER *suddenly holds out an arm to* PEEL.

Penner : David, David boy—it wasn't the truth——

Peel (*tending him*) : There, there, it's all right.

Penner : No—the doctor was wrong—I'm——

Peel (*lifting him into his arms*) : Duff, it will go in a minute, don't be frightened.

Penner : No. I'm not frightened. I'm dying.

Warrenton (*to Peel*) : What can we do ?

Penner : Good-bye, Ray, old fellow—good-bye,

David—we've had great times—I wish I could have
seen General Lee, say good-bye to him for me.
Give my love to old Tom.

> *He falls back in* PEEL's *arms, and dies.*

Peel (*passionately*): Duff—Duff—Duff. He's dead.
Just thrown away—a little warmth and attention
could have done it, and he couldn't have them.

Warrenton: He saved my life—that day at
Frazier's—and I could do nothing but sit here useless
hour after hour. He was a great old Duff. After
four years . . .

Peel: There's no bitterness for him now.

> *Very tenderly he covers* PENNER'S *body and
> face with the coat.*

Warrenton: Bitterness? We are too tired.

Peel: That is what we shall have to fight now, in
ourselves, in our children, perhaps. Just lean, dull
days are coming—they breed it.

Warrenton: You said we should have to build—on
a memory.

Peel: If we can keep the memory a clean one.
Duff won't know that struggle.

> LEE *comes in slowly, followed by his* AIDE *and*
> BUCHANAN. PEEL *and* WARRENTON *stand at
> attention.*

Lee: You needn't do that. Rest. (*Seeing* PENNER'S
body) What's this?

Peel: He's dead, sir. He wanted to say good-bye
to you.

> LEE *stands silently by the body for a moment,
> then speaks to the* AIDE.

Lee : I'll just finish that report.   Will you wait, Tom ?   I want you to take down an order directly.

He goes into the tent, followed by the AIDE.

Buchanan (*kneeling by* PENNER) : Duff, old friend.

Warrenton : He sent his love to you.

Buchanan : He hadn't a fair chance.

Peel : We could do nothing.

Buchanan (*standing up*) : Well, it's all over.

Peel : What happened ?

Buchanan : The General was superb.   No political matters were mentioned.   Grant behaved very well. But we've lost pretty near everything, David.

Warrenton : What are we to do ?

Buchanan : I think we are to go home.

Warrenton : Home.   There isn't a Mount Weston any more.   Sherman has been there.

Peel : Did the General say anything, afterwards ?

Buchanan : Not a word all the way back.

Warrenton : Do you think he knows how much we love him ?

Buchanan : I'm sure he does, and yet he's terribly alone.

Peel : The story that you are going to be doesn't help much, does it ?   His Mount Westons are so many, Ray.   It's almost like . . .

Warrenton : I know.

Buchanan : Rations are to be served at six o'clock this evening.   Full rations.

Peel : The funeral baked meats.

Warrenton : I'll go and get them to move Duff.

He goes.

LEE *comes to the tent opening.*

Lee: That will do. Take it at once, will you, please?

The AIDE *comes from the tent, carrying his papers, and goes.*

Lee (*after walking two or three times up and down in front of the tent*): It's getting warm again. Almost like that night at Arlington, four years ago. (*Again he walks to and fro, silently.*) Tom, will you take this down, please?

BUCHANAN *goes into the tent.*

Peel: Shall I go, sir?

Lee: No. It's for everybody.

BUCHANAN *brings a seat to the tent opening and sits with pencil and paper.* PEEL *sits beside* PENNER'S *body.*

Lee (*dictating as he walks*): ' Headquarters Army of Northern Virginia. April 10th, 1865. General Order No. 9. After four years of arduous service marked by unsurpassed courage and fortitude, the Army of Northern Virginia has been compelled to yield to overwhelming numbers and resources.

' I need not tell the survivors of so many hard-fought battles who have remained steadfast to the last that I have consented to this result from no distrust of them ; but feeling that valour and devotion could accomplish nothing that would compensate for the loss that must have attended the continuance of the contest, I determined to avoid useless sacrifice of those whose past services have endeared them to their countrymen. By the terms of the agreement, officers and men can return to their homes and remain until exchanged.

'You may take with you the satisfaction that proceeds from the consciousness of duty faithfully performed, and I earnestly pray that a merciful God will extend to you His blessing and protection.

'With an unceasing admiration of your constancy and devotion to your country, and a grateful remembrance of your kind and generous consideration of myself, I bid you all an affectionate farewell.'

> *He stands still as he finishes,* BUCHANAN *goes into the tent. Daylight is going.*

Peel (*standing up*): You know, sir, we would have gone on for you.

Lee: My boy.

Peel: Yes, sir—clothes and food and boots didn't matter—we would have gone on.

Lee: I know. I have seen it. But it couldn't have changed anything. We should have dwindled away, and there wouldn't have been even this little waif of an army to send back. There is other service now. (*Moving to* PENNER) Poor Duff.

Peel: I think so often of what you said that night at Arlington, sir. 'You may be wiser than Virginia,' you said, 'but your wisdom doesn't matter till she doesn't need you any more in her quarrel.' Is the quarrel over now, sir?

Lee: To learn that, to teach it—that is the other service. Duff and his thousands have given their all for the quarrel. They have died for Virginia. We live, and again we are just Virginians no longer. We were that, and we, too, would have died for it. But we have now to live for America.

Peel: But will they let us?

Lee : We asked no leave four years ago—we shall ask none now. We believed in ourselves. The answer has been given. But we have the courage still that we had then. We used it for Virginia— we shall use it for America. We have no choice —I do not think that we now should ask or want any. We can only build our South again, and find our own hearts, in that service. We had a loyalty, we have a loyalty. Virginia knows us, she will know us for ever. But we are Americans once more. We must not dispute about it.

Peel : I see, yes—to learn and to teach.

BUCHANAN *comes from the tent, a paper in his hand.*

Buchanan : Will you read that over, sir.

Lee : Yes. Thank you.

He takes the paper and goes into the tent.

Peel : If he could speak to every man in this land of ours.

Buchanan : He will.

After a moment, WARRENTON *comes back.*

Warrenton : They are coming to fetch Duff.

It is now dusk. A light comes from the tent.

Peel : The dead, and a memory, and a hope. A name—Robert E. Lee. To-morrow we are going home. (*He takes their hands.*) He is going with us.

As they stand by PENNER'S *body*

THE SCENE CLOSES.

THE END.

The first production of *Robert E. Lee* was at the Regent Theatre, London, on Wednesday, June 20, 1923, under the direction of the Author and Nigel Playfair, with the following cast:—

Major Perrin	HARVEY ADAMS
An Orderly	GEOFFREY WILKINSO N
General Scott	F. KINSEY PEILE
Robert E. Lee	FELIX AYLMER
Tom Buchanan	TRISTAN RAWSON
Ray Warrenton	HAROLD ANSTRUT H ER
David Peel	CLAUDE RAINS
Duff Penner	HENRY CAINE
John Stean	ATHOLL DOUGLAS
A Girl	ANN HYTON
Mrs. Stean	MARGOT SIEVEKING
A Servant	GEOFFREY WINCOTT
General J. E. B. Stuart	LEO G. CARROLL
His Aide	GEOFFREY WINCOTT
An Aide to General Lee	JOHN GIELGUD
A Sentry	FRANK MARTIN
Captain Mason	ATHOLL DOUGLAS
Captain Udall	MAURICE BRADDELL
General Stonewall Jackson	EDMUND WILLARD
Colonel Hewitt	HARVEY ADAMS
Jefferson Davis	GORDON HARKER
His Secretary	GEOFFREY WILKINSON
Mrs. Meadows	NATALIE LYNN

The scenes and costumes were designed by Doris Zinkeisen and the stage management was in the hands of Stephen Thomas.